WordPress For Beginners

A Visual Guide To Building Your
WordPress Site

+

22 Top WordPress Plugins

NATHAN GEORGE

CONTENTS

CONTENTS

INTRODUCTION

WordPress is a Content Management System (CMS) that makes it easy to create a website with any kind of functionality you want easily. Before applications like WordPress were available, if you wanted to create a website, you would need to have some web design skills, or you would need to hire a web developer to design it for you. With the advent of tools like WordPress, it is now much easier for someone without web design skills to create a fully functional website within a few minutes.

WordPress is an open source application which started as a blog engine but has blown into a fully functional CMS. By open source, it means nobody owns it hence a group of people from all over the world can work on it and continually improve it. For this reason, WordPress has managed to remain free even though it is constantly being upgraded and improved.

WordPress is referred to as a publishing platform because it is not just a blogging tool. Many large online companies and agencies now use WordPress to run their sites. For example, the New York Times, Wall Street Journal, Forbes etc. all use WordPress as the tool for their publishing platforms.

You can use WordPress to run sites with relatively static content or sites with dynamic content organised in chronological order.

You can use WordPress for the following sites:

- E-commerce stores
- Corporate websites
- Membership sites

- Product websites
- Regular blogs
- Photoblogs
- Video blogs

WordPress is a web application and hence needs to be installed on a web server, which is usually a remote computer.

Who Is This Book For?

This book is for you if you are new to WordPress or looking to create a website for the first time and don't know where to start. This book will hold your hands in helping you to get your first website up and running even if you're a complete beginner. We will start from the very beginning - getting a domain name registered and a hosting account before moving on to installing WordPress and creating your website.

After reading this book, you will have all the knowledge you need to create your first WordPress website, install themes, plugins, create menus, and create widgets.

Even if you already have some experience with WordPress this book also covers some advanced topics that you may find invaluable in maintaining your WordPress site. For example, we cover how to manually backup your WordPress contents folder and your MySQL database. This ensures you have flexibility and not dependent on plugins that can sometimes be unreliable.

CHAPTER 1: USING WORDPRESS.COM

1.1 Using WordPress.com

The first decision you'll need to make is where your website is going to be hosted. WordPress.org is where you download WordPress for installation on a remote server. WordPress.com, on the other hand, is a free platform where you can create your website for free on the Internet.

With WordPress you have two basic options:

1. Create a free WordPress site - Wordpress.com

2. Install WordPress on a remote server – WordPress.org

This book will focus primarily on the second option (installing WordPress on a remote web host) however in this chapter I'll briefly cover WordPress.com for those interested in exploring this free platform. If you have no interest in using WordPress.com then you can skip this chapter.

WordPress.com started as a free a platform provided by WordPress that enables you to create a website that is hosted on their server. It has since expanded to providing additional packages which are paid options that enable you to have more features.

In this chapter, we'll be discussing the free option. The main problem with the free option is that you would be restricted regarding the level of customisation you can carry out on WordPress. Below we'll examine some advantages and disadvantages of using WordPress.com

Pros:

- You can host your website for free.
- They take care of all technical details for you.
- The software is installed already.
- They will upgrade WordPress for you whenever there is an upgrade.
- Response times when designing your website may be faster compared to one of the shared starter packages with a hosting provider.
- The paid plans give you more freedom like having your own domain name, installing premium themes, integrating with third party tools like Google Analytics etc.

Cons:

- The free plan does not allow you to have your own domain name.
- The free plan does not allow you to install your own themes and plugins. You're limited to the themes and plugins they provide.
- Some plugins are installed by default which you cannot remove.
- You cannot integrate your site with third party tools like Google Analytics, unless you get the Business plan.
- The Premium and Business plans give you a bit more freedom but they're pricey compared to the average starter package from a hosting provider.

The major advantage of hosting WordPress on your own server account (which means a remote server on the Internet) is that you have control of everything. You can add and edit themes. You can add and remove whichever plugins you want. You can even edit WordPress at the code level if you have some PHP skills (although that is becoming increasingly unnecessary as you can get a plugin for almost any functionality now).

Apart from the cost of hosting your own WordPress site, one disadvantage is that you have to install and maintain your WordPress site yourself. You have to keep WordPress and all installed plugins up to date yourself. Thankfully that is getting easier as you can now set WordPress and some plugins to automatically update themselves whenever there are new versions.

One reason to use WordPress.com is if you want a relatively quick and simple website. For example, you might be an author and you just need a quick website for one of your pen names to list your books. In that case, you may want something simple, without any bells and whistles. In those situations it may not be worthwhile to get a paid account with a web host if WordPress.com can meet your needs.

How to create a blog on WordPress.com

WordPress.com is provided by WordPress developers and you can register a new blog very easily with no hassles.

You first need to create an account with **wordpress.com** before you can begin to create websites. You can have several blogs if you so choose and you can manage them from your home page, once you have created them.

Once you've created your account you will get the option to add a site.

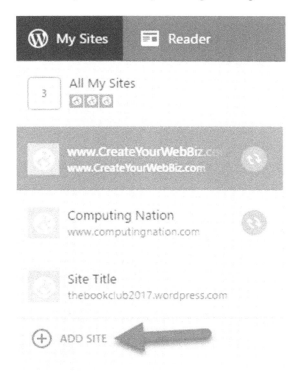

When you click on ADD SITE on your homepage, you will get the option to add a new WordPress.com site or a WordPress.org site hosted elsewhere. Choose New WordPress.com to get to the next screen which will give you options to choose the layout of your home page.

Step 1. If you want a blog you would choose option one. If you want a static landing page, choose option two. If you want a grid showing your latest posts then you should choose option three.

Step 2. You can choose your theme from a few options provided. These themes are free and adequate for a basic site. Click on one and move to the next page.

Step 3. The next screen enables you to choose your domain name, which will have wordpress.com appended to it. So it will be a subdomain of wordpress.com. If you have your own domain name, for example, www.mysite.com then you can use it here for the premium version of WordPress.com. The cost of the premium version of WordPress.com at the time of this writing is about $9/month or $99/year.

On the next screen, you get various packages to choose from ranging from a free package to a paid business package. If you're going for the free package you simply click on Select.

The site is then created for you and you are taken to your homepage where you can start configuring your site and entering posts.

As you can see, creating a WordPress.com site is pretty quick and straightforward. This is ideal if you need something basic that is responsive and free. For anything more complex like a business site, where you want more control of themes and plugins, you'll need to install WordPress on a web host.

CHAPTER 2: GETTING STARTED WITH WORDPRESS.ORG

2.1 Choosing and Registering Your Domain Name

One of the first things you need for a website is to decide on your domain name. Your **domain name** is the web address that people can use to find your site, for example *www.mysite.com*. Domain names are unique, meaning you are the only one who would have this name on the internet.

If your WordPress site is a personal blog, then you're probably using a combination of your name to create your domain name hence it is more likely to be unique. However, if you're using your WordPress site for commercial purposes and your name is made up of more general terms, then you need to ensure the name is free and available before you try to register it.

There is a great free tool online provided by Shopify that you can use to brainstorm available domain names. You're not using Shopify for your site. This is just a free tool they offer that anyone can use to check for available domain names.

https://www.shopify.co.uk/tools/business-name-generator

You just enter the main keywords for your blog, or the name of your company and it will give you different combinations of available domain names.

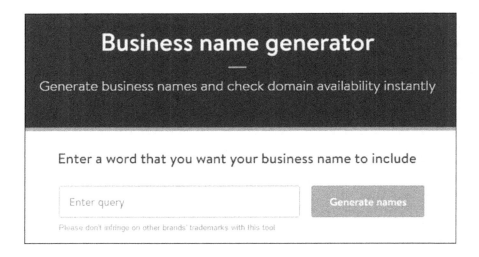

Registering Your Domain Name

Once you've decided on a domain name, you've got two options:

1. If you're purchasing a new hosting package, most web hosts offer a free domain to go with your package. So, you can register your domain name for free at the same time as you sign up for your hosting package.

2. If you already have a web host, you should register your domain name with a dedicated **Domain Registrar**. This should ideally be separate from your web host. It is a good idea to keep them separate so that if you have

any problems with your web host, and you decide to switch companies, you do not want your domain name affected as well.

I currently use **Namecheap** to register most of my domain names but there are some other popular options out there like **GoDaddy** for example. You need to shop around for the best price from a reputable domain registrar. I have found Namecheap to offer very competitive rates and they provide a very user-friendly admin dashboard for managing your domain names.

If your website is a business, it is advisable to go for a **.com** domain unless you have specific reasons to choose another top-level domain. Most people typing in your website address will assume it ends with a .com and it's easier for people to remember.

If your website is a personal blog then having a .com domain is not so important. You may also be creating a website in a specific industry that uses a particular top-level domain like **.org** or **.net**, for example, so you may want to follow the same convention.

A .com domain name from Namecheap or Go Daddy will usually cost between $6.99 and $10.99 annually. You'll have the option of manually renewing your domain name every year or setting it to auto-renew on your dashboard.

NameCheap: https://www.namecheap.com/

GoDaddy: https://www.godaddy.com/

2.2 Choosing a Web Host

A web host provides a server on the Internet that hosts your website. This ensures your site is available 24/7, and the web host deals with all availability and maintenance issues. So, you're essentially outsourcing the hosting of your website to a web hosting service.

Hosting Type

As a WordPress beginner you have two main hosting options:

Shared hosting

With a shared hosting account, you share server resources with several other websites. You're responsible for installing and managing WordPress (or even any other CMS software the host supports). Tweaking, optimising and securing your website is left to you.

Managed WordPress

Managed WordPress is optimised for WordPress hosting. They manage everything including speed, security and support. Hence managed WordPress is usually more expensive than shared hosting. For example, at Bluehost, the managed WordPress packages start at $19.99 per month while the shared package starts at around $5.00 per month.

If you are installing WordPress for commercial purposes, then the managed WordPress option is more suitable. If you can afford the cost upfront, it is the best option to start with. However, if you can't afford managed WordPress, then a shared package is an OK place to start in gaining experience running a website on the internet for little cost.

If you're new to WordPress and creating a personal blog, then I would suggest starting with a shared hosting package. If your blog grows in future and starts generating a lot of traffic, you may consider moving to a better hosting package.

Hosting Companies

There are several web hosting providers out there and you should do your research first before choosing one. Keep in mind that some domain registrars also provide web hosting services, but they are better at being domain registrars and not web hosts, for example, GoDaddy and Namecheap.

Below are some providers I have used in the past or know people who have used them and speak well of them.

Shared hosting options ($5.00 per month or less):

1. **Bluehost: -** This is one of the popular hosting options for people new to shared hosting packages. They also have a series of managed WordPress plans ranging from Standard to Ultimate.

   Link: www.Bluehost.com

2. **SiteGround:** This is another popular hosting option for beginners. They have a series of shared hosting plans for different needs.

   Link: www.Siteground.com

Managed WordPress options ($25.00 per month or less):

1. **WPX Hosting:** This provider is dedicated to managed WordPress and slightly pricier than the other providers. However, the speed you get at the backend when designing your site in WP Admin can be worth the extra cost.

   Link: https://wpxhosting.com/

2. **Flywheel:** This is another provider dedicated to managed WordPress. They offer a basic starting package of $14.00 per month which may be good for a beginner.

   Link: https://getflywheel.com/

Addon Domains (Shared Hosting)

If you are getting a shared hosting package, like the ones from Bluehost or SiteGround, for example, always ensure you go for a package that allows you to have unlimited websites. These are called **addon domains** which are different from subdomains. It doesn't cost that much more to get a package that allows multiple websites and it may save you a lot of headache down the line if you want to host another website.

Addon domains enable you to add multiple websites to the same web hosting account using standalone domain names, for example, *www.mysecondsite.com*.

So, you're not forced to use subdomains that are prefixed to your main domain, for example, *mysecondsite.createyourwebbiz.com*. On many occasions when you want to create another site you want a new standalone domain name and not a name that is prefixed to your current domain.

You can start with a shared package that offers unlimited websites (like the $5.95/month package in the example below). If you're finding it too slow for your business needs at some point, you can upgrade You can upgrade at any time and they would usually credit any unused subscription towards your new package.

	Basic	Plus	Prime
			Recommended
	normally $7.99	normally $9.99	normally $14.99
	$2.95*/mo ✗	$5.95*/mo ✓	$5.95*/mo ✓
	Select	Select	Select
Websites	1	Unlimited	Unlimited
Website Space	50 GB	Unmetered	Unmetered
Bandwidth	Unmetered	Unmetered	Unmetered

Linking Your Domain Name To Your Hosting Account

When you register your domain with a different registrar from your web host you'll need to link your domain name to the nameservers of your web host.

Your web host will send you details of their nameservers after you sign up with them. You now need to go to your domain registrar, login to your dashboard, and update the nameserver fields to the server names provided by your web host. The way you do this may vary depending on your domain registrar, but you'll find instructions by searching the help section at your domain registrar.

This ensures that when people type in your domain name on the Internet it resolves to the servers at your web host.

2.3 Installing WordPress With An Auto Installer

The following information is based on a shared hosting package. Once you've sorted out your domain name and web host, you now need to install WordPress. You can choose to install WordPress manually or use the auto installer provided by your web host. I'll be covering both methods in this book.

In this chapter, we'll cover how you can install WordPress very quickly using the auto installer provided on **cPanel**.

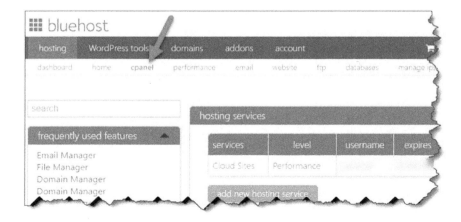

On cPanel (or the admin panel of your web host), you'll see a button to install WordPress with the group of icons under **website**.

Click on the **Install WordPress** icon to start the WordPress installation process. It takes you to the next screen where you need to enter the domain name of your website.

Enter the domain name you registered for this website and click on **Next**.

On the next screen, you're presented with fields to enter your Site Name or Title, Admin Username, Admin Email Address, and Admin Password.

Enter the values and click on **Install**. The script will go to work in creating a MySQL database and installing a copy of WordPress to create your site.

The whole process may take no more than 5 minutes from start to finish and you would have your website up and running. Once installed you'll be taken to the admin login screen so that you can log in to the **WP Admin** panel where you can start customising your site.

2.4 How To Install WordPress Manually

Step 1: Create The MySQL Database

Note that depending on your web host you may have different screens for carrying out these tasks however the underlying process is the same. For the following example, I'll be using an account on BlueHost.

On cPanel, click on **MySQL Databases** to create a new MySQL database for the site.

On the next screen, enter your database name. The database name will be created by prefixing it with the username you use to login to your hosting account. For example, *myusername_wptestsite*.

You now need to create a user and give the user full access to the new database.

After creating the User add them to the database.

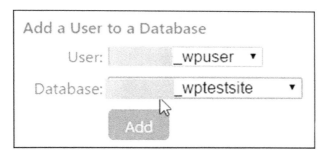

Assign the user full rights access to the database you have just created.

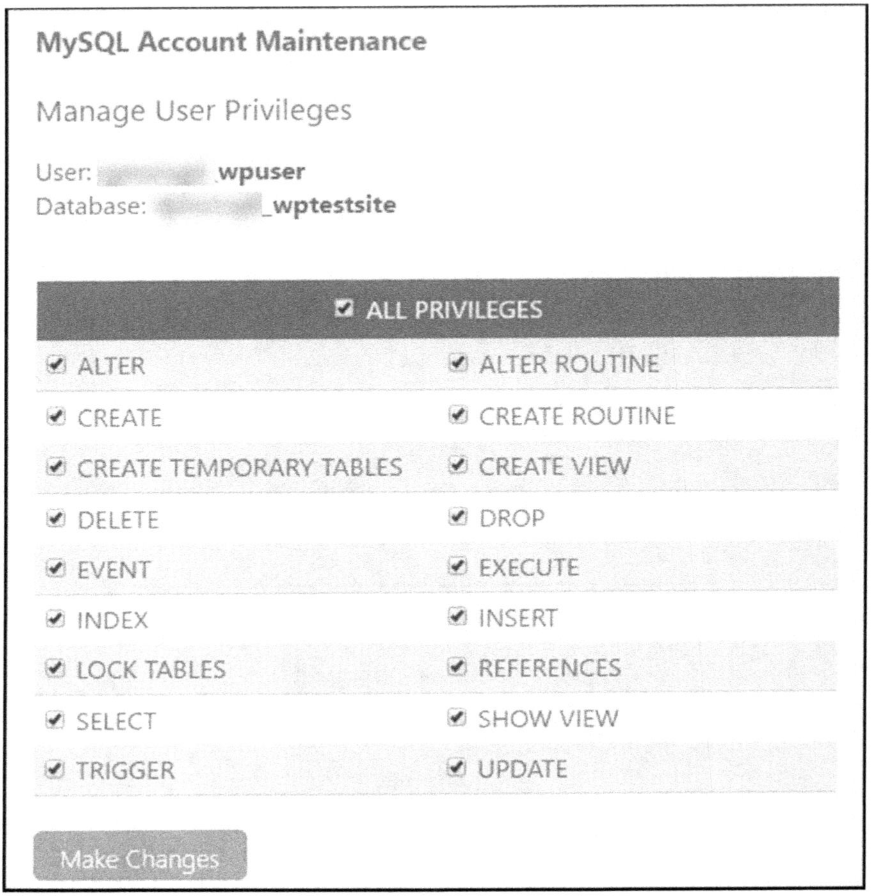

MySQL Account Maintenance

Manage User Privileges

User: ███████ _wpuser
Database: ███████ _wptestsite

☑ ALL PRIVILEGES	
☑ ALTER	☑ ALTER ROUTINE
☑ CREATE	☑ CREATE ROUTINE
☑ CREATE TEMPORARY TABLES	☑ CREATE VIEW
☑ DELETE	☑ DROP
☑ EVENT	☑ EXECUTE
☑ INDEX	☑ INSERT
☑ LOCK TABLES	☑ REFERENCES
☑ SELECT	☑ SHOW VIEW
☑ TRIGGER	☑ UPDATE

Make Changes

With that, you have created the database needed for your WordPress site. Next you need to download and install the WordPress application.

Step 2: Download And Copy The WordPress Application Folder To Your Web Host

Download the latest version of WordPress from **https://wordpress.org/** and unzip the file to a directory on your PC.

Log in to the admin panel of your web host (or cPanel) and launch File Manager.

Upload the zipped file you downloaded from WordPress.org to a temp directory on the root of your account, and then extract the file using the Extract function provided by **File Manager**.

After extracting the file, copy the contents of the **wordpress** folder into your Web Root, which is usually named **public_html**. The contents of the wordpress folder are usually made up of 3 folders: **wp-admin**, **wp-content**, **wp-includes** and a series of files.

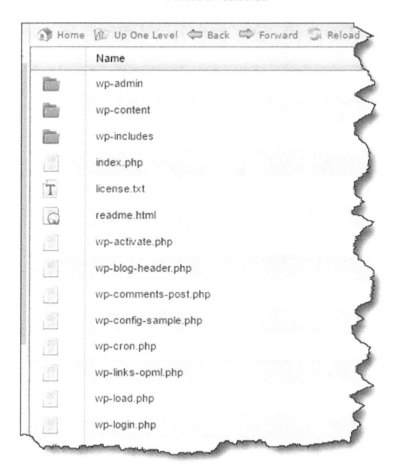

Select all items in the wordpress folder and use the **Copy** function in File Manager to copy them into public_html (or the folder you're using for your website if you're using an addon domain). Alternatively, you can select them and then drag and drop them into public_html.

Step 3: Update wp-config.php With Your Database Login Details

The contents of the wordpress folder include 3 folders and a series of files which include wp-config-sample.php.

Make a copy of wp-config-sample.php in your web root and name it **wp-config.php**.

Right click on **wp-config.php** and click on edit. The file will be opened in a file editor. You need to update the following fields with your database name and user login credentials that you created previously:

- DB_NAME

- DB_USER

- DB_PASSWORD

You'll find these fields in a section of the file that looks like this:
// ** MySQL settings - You can get this info from your web host ** //

/** The name of the database for WordPress */
define('**DB_NAME**', '*accountname_wptestsite*');

/** MySQL database username */
define('**DB_USER**', '*accountname_wpuser*');

/** MySQL database password */
define('**DB_PASSWORD**', '*yourpassword*');

Next, for security purposes you need to define some unique keys for your website. These secret keys are used by WordPress to add random characters to passwords and they're also used in many other security situations. This adds a level of protection to your site that makes it harder for someone to hack into it.

You can get secret keys generated for you by going to:

https://api.wordpress.org/secret-key/1.1/salt/

Copy the link and paste it in the address bar of your web browser, and then press enter.

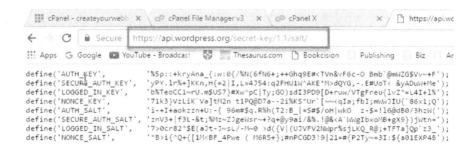

You get a unique set of keys which you should copy and paste in your **wp-config.php** file. The keys should replace the section of the file with placeholders for these keys.

```
define('AUTH_KEY',         'put your unique phrase here');
define('SECURE_AUTH_KEY', 'put your unique phrase here');
define('LOGGED_IN_KEY',    'put your unique phrase here');
define('NONCE_KEY',        'put your unique phrase here');
define('AUTH_SALT',        'put your unique phrase here');
define('SECURE_AUTH_SALT', 'put your unique phrase here');
define('LOGGED_IN_SALT',   'put your unique phrase here');
define('NONCE_SALT',       'put your unique phrase here');
```

Save the **wp-config.php** file and close File Manager.

Step 4: Launch The Installation Process

Launch your web browser and type in your domain name in the address bar. This will launch the WordPress installation screen (if all the previous steps have been carried out properly).

Note: If you get an error page at this point, instead of the installation page, review your wp-config.php file and ensure all values have been entered correctly. If all is OK with the wp-config.php file and you're still getting an error, review all the previous steps to ensure they've all been carried out as explained here.

If all is OK you should get the installation page where you can now enter your site title and login details.

Welcome

Welcome to the famous five-minute WordPress installation process! Just fill in the information below and you'll be on your way to using the most extendable and powerful personal publishing platform in the world.

Information needed

Please provide the following information. Don't worry, you can always change these settings later.

Site Title

Username

Usernames can have only alphanumeric characters, spaces, underscores, hyphens, full stops, and the @ symbol.

Password   👁 Show

Important: You will need this password to log in. Please store it in a secure location.

Your Email

Double-check your email address before continuing.

Search Engine Visibility   ☐ Discourage search engines from indexing this site
It is up to search engines to honour this request.

Install WordPress

Enter the values and click on **Install WordPress** to install the program. Once done you'll be taken to the WP Admin login screen where you can log in and start customising your site.

CHAPTER 3: CREATING CONTENT

3.1 The WP Admin Panel

WordPress installs a powerful and flexible admin area which is the engine room of your WordPress site. WP Admin allows you to manage your content and configure the settings on your site. For the rest of this book, I will be referring to it as WP Admin.

To access the WP Admin panel of your site you go to:

http://www.yoursite.com/wp-admin/

The first time you access it, you will be directed to the login page. To log in, you need to enter the username and password that you chose during the installation of WordPress. When you log in you will be taken to the dashboard of WP Admin.

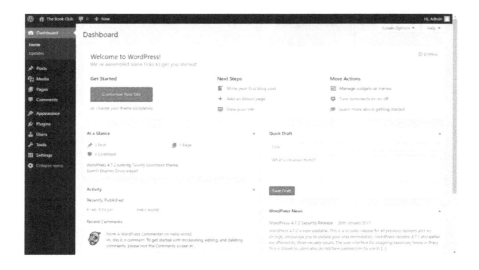

At the top of the screen, you have a tab named **Screen Options** which appears on several screens in WP Admin. When you click on it, it will slide down to show you a contextual list of options relating to the page that you're viewing. So you can check or uncheck items on the list to change what is displayed on the page.

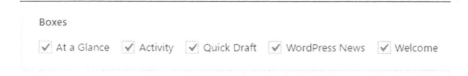

Next to Screen Options is the **Help** tab. The help provided is also contextual and will change depending on which page you're viewing. Click on Help for explanations on what each field on the screen you're viewing represents, and what actions can be carried out on them.

On the left side of the screen, you have the main menu. You can click on any of the items on the main menu to expand it and display the sub-items.

You can also hover over a main menu item with your mouse to get a pop out list of the sub-items.

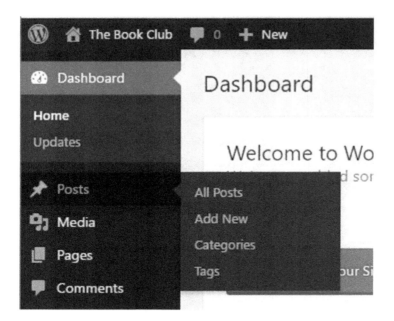

Configuring Post Settings

One of the first things you'll need to do is configure the settings for your site.

Click on **Settings** to expand the group, then click on **General** to show the **General Settings** screen.

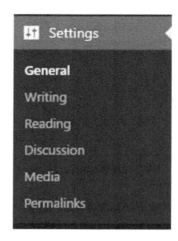

On the **General Settings** screen enter your Site Title, Tagline, and any other values you want to change from the default, like Timezone for example. Then click on **Save Changes**.

Under **Settings** click on **Reading** to display the **Reading Settings** screen. Here you can set how the front page is displayed. You can leave it as the default which is your latest posts or set it to a static page which you can select from a list (if you've created a page you want to use as your static front page).

You can also set how many blog posts you want shown at the most. The default is 10 posts.

Under **Settings** click on **Permalink** to access the **Permalink Settings** page. You want to set your permalinks to **Post name** so that the title of your post is used for your web links instead of the date.

Common Settings

Plain	http://localhost/thebookclub/?p=123
Day and name	http://localhost/thebookclub/2017/02/12/sample-post/
Month and name	http://localhost/thebookclub/2017/02/sample-post/
Numeric	http://localhost/thebookclub/archives/123
● Post name	http://localhost/thebookclub/sample-post/

Click on **Save Changes** when you're done.

3.2 Creating and Editing Posts

Each entry in the blog is called a post. Each post, at the least, would have a title and the content. You may also have images and links in your posts. Every post has a publication timestamp and you can also assign categories and tags when you create them.

The posts are displayed in chronological order on the main page of your blog. The latest posts are displayed first by default so that viewers can see the latest content on the blog.

To add a new post, from the main menu click on **Posts**, then **Add New**. You'll get the **Add a New Post** screen. Enter the title of the post and the content using the WP editor.

You can click on the "kitchen sink" icon to toggle the toolbar to show more formatting icons.

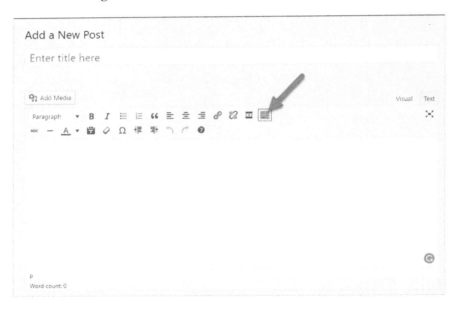

To see the HTML code for the content, click on the **Text** tab. This is useful if you have some formatting issues in the Visual view and you cannot find the source of it. When you switch to Text view you can see exactly how each paragraph is being formatted in HTML and if there is any code there causing a problem.

To add images to your content click on the **Add Media** button to display the **Insert Media** screen. You can select images from your Media Library (if you've uploaded images previously) or you can upload an image by clicking on the **Upload Files** tab and then the **Select Files** button.

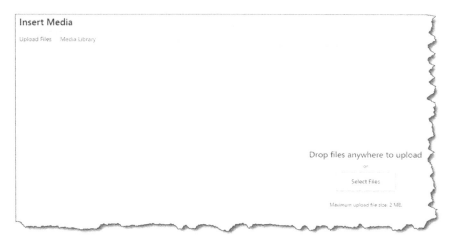

When you upload an image you are taken to the **Media Library** where the image is displayed. On the right side of the screen, you see the properties of the picture.

The **Attachment Display Settings** enables you to set the alignment, add a web link, and adjust the size of the image.

3.3 Categories, Tags and Featured Images

On the right-hand side of the **Add a New Post** screen, you'll find a series of boxes which include **Publish, Format, Categories, Tags** and **Featured Image**.

Publish enables you to save the post as a draft for later or to publish it and make it live.

Format provides several options for displaying your post. The default is the standard format which is used for most text with attached images. You can explore the other formats if you want a different kind of layout. See Help for a description of each format.

Categories and **Tags** offer a way to organise the content on your site so that your posts are easy to find. Categories are akin to topics while tags are more like keywords that you can attach to each post. For example, a blog about food could have a category called *breakfast* and tags like *eggs, toast, low-fat, tomatoes* etc.

In the **Categories** box, you have *Uncategorised* as the default. Click on **Add New Category** to add a new category to your site. When you add a new category it will become available for selection for all future posts.

To add tags, in the **Tags** box, type in a tag you want to attach to your post and click **Add**. You can add as many tags as you want to a post. If you have entered tags previously then you'll be able to choose from a list of the most used tags.

The **Featured Image** box enables you to choose an image to go with your post. How the image is displayed with the post depends on the style of the theme you've installed. Different WordPress themes have different ways of displaying the featured image, however, this is the place where you set the image.

3.4 Creating and Editing Pages

The screen used to create pages is very similar to the one used to create posts in that they both have the title and the content area where you can write your text and add images or videos. However, pages do not have categories or tags. Posts show up on your blog page in chronological order. Pages on the other hand are standalone and you should treat them as static pieces of content.

Pages are meant to hold content that's always up to date and relevant whereas posts are more time sensitive in that they provide advice or news that's current today.

When you install WordPress for the first time a sample page is automatically created for you.

To add a new page, from WP Admin, click on **Pages** and then **Add New**. You'll get a screen similar to the **Add Post** screen with the WordPress editor.

The minimum you need to do to create a new page is to enter the title and some content. Then you click on the **Publish** button and your new page will become available under its unique URL.

Under **Page Attributes**, on the right-side of the screen, WordPress allows you to arrange your pages hierarchically. This enables you to organise your content into pages and subpages, especially if you intend to have a lot of pages.

Under Page Attributes, you can select a **Parent** page for the current page you're creating. For example, you may have a page for *Meals* and make that the parent page for another page - *Breakfast* and it will be displayed as a subpage of *Meals* on your menu.

Like a post, you can also add a featured image to your pages using the **Featured Image** box.

3.5 Adding Media

You can upload images to your site at the same time as you add posts and pages. You can also upload images directly to your site's media library using the **Media** menu item in **WP Admin**.

To add images to your site, from the main menu click on **Media** and **Add New**.

Drag and drop files from your computer onto the area with the dotted line or click on **Select Files** to launch a dialogue box that enables you to select files to upload.

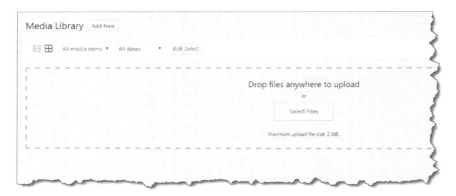

If you wish to adjust an image you've uploaded, click on the image to launch the **Attachment Details** screen, and then click on the **Edit Image** button to edit the image.

CHAPTER 4: DESIGN AND LAYOUT

4.1 Installing Free Themes

One of the great advantages of using a Content Management System (CMS) like WordPress is that you can quickly change the look and feel of your site without coding skills or your content being affected. There are thousands of WordPress themes available to download for free and thousands more you can buy at a pretty low cost.

To find free WordPress themes for your site go to **wordpress.org**:

https://wordpress.org/themes/

This is where providers of free themes in the WordPress community upload their free themes for anyone to download. They tag them with keywords and provide a description of the basic look, layout, and function of the theme. You can also view a demo of the theme before you download it.

When you download a free theme ensure you get the ones that are up to date. You can check the date by looking at the **Last updated** field. If this date is too far in the past then there is a risk the theme may no longer be compatible with the latest release of WordPress as it is constantly being updated.

You can also access this site from within WP Admin. In WP Admin, click on **Appearance** and then click on **Themes**.

Click on **Add New** to go to the Add Themes page. Here you can select one of the free themes from the options available or upload a new theme. You can explore the categories listed clicking on *Featured, Popular, Latest,* and *Favourites.*

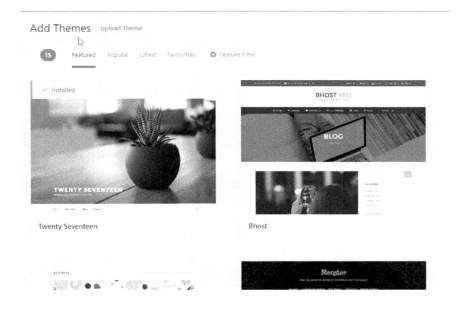

Click on **Feature Filter** to display a list of filters from 3 categories (Layout, Features and Subject) that enable you to narrow down the results.

After selecting your filter options, click on **Apply Filters** to get a filtered list.

To install one of the free themes hover your mouse over it and click on **More Info** to view more details or you can click on **Install** to install it right away.

Take note that free themes are usually basic in functionality and they may not always be kept up to date with WordPress updates. For example, your site could suddenly stop working properly after new WordPress release if the theme designer does not update it.

If you want to use your site for basic blogging then a free theme might suffice. However, if you're using your site for business, it is recommended that you get a premium theme.

4.2 Installing Premium Themes

If you intend to use your site for commercial purposes then you would likely want to get a premium theme installed. Premium themes are usually kept up to date with the latest release of WordPress. So if a new version of WordPress is released and your site's layout breaks, you could go to your theme provider and download the latest release which would have been updated to fix any incompatibility issues. On most occasions, you would simply get a message on your dashboard that an update for your theme is available for installation.

The price of premium themes ranges from $30 - $100 depending on the provider and the features provided. There are usually two modes of licensing. You can buy a *standard licence* for personal sites or a *developer license* that allows you to use the theme on client sites if you are a web developer.

Ensure you choose a theme that is appropriate for the kind of site you want to create. There are different types of themes. For example, traditional blogs, photo blogs, video blogs, corporate sites, e-commerce sites, and online magazines. Most of the premium theme providers provide filters that enable you to narrow down their list and show only themes that match your criteria.

Also, always go for themes that are fully responsive. That is, they would adjust for any browser or device, e.g. a tablet, e-reader or smartphone. People access the internet with all kinds of devices these days and it is important that your website is compatible with all devices people use to browse the internet.

To get a premium theme here are a few recommendations:

StudioPress: http://www.studiopress.com/

Thrive Themes: https://thrivethemes.com/themes/

WooThemes: https://woocommerce.com/woothemes/

ThemeForest: https://themeforest.net/category/wordpress

Premium theme providers usually provide support and documentation for their themes so when you buy a premium theme you would have instructions on how to configure the settings for your site.

To install a premium theme, first, download the zip file from the provider's website. Then go to **WP Admin => Appearance => Themes**. Click on **Add New => Upload Theme => Choose File** to select the zip file that you downloaded from your theme provider and then click on **Install Now**.

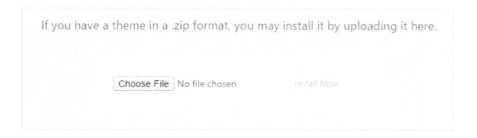

Configuring Your Premium Theme Settings

When you install your theme you'll get a few more items on your WP Admin menu related to your theme. Most of your site's layout and style e.g. header, background colour, text fonts, layout etc. would be configured from within the settings panel of the theme.

4.3 How to Create Menus

Menus are used for navigating your website. The WordPress menu feature allows you to create menus with links to pages, category archives, and even URLs to other websites. After creating your menus you can place them at the top or the bottom of your page.

Before you start creating a menu you should first create the pages that you want to appear on the menu. To add a menu to your site, in WP Admin, click on **Appearance**, then **Menus** to display the **Menus** page.

On the left side of the screen, you'll see the following menu item types: **Pages**, **Posts**, **Custom Links**, and **Categories**. To create a new menu, enter the name in the **Menu Name** field and click on **Create Menu**.

The menu will be created and you'll get a new screen that enables you to add the items you want to the menu. You can add items by selecting them on the left-hand side and clicking on **Add to Menu**.

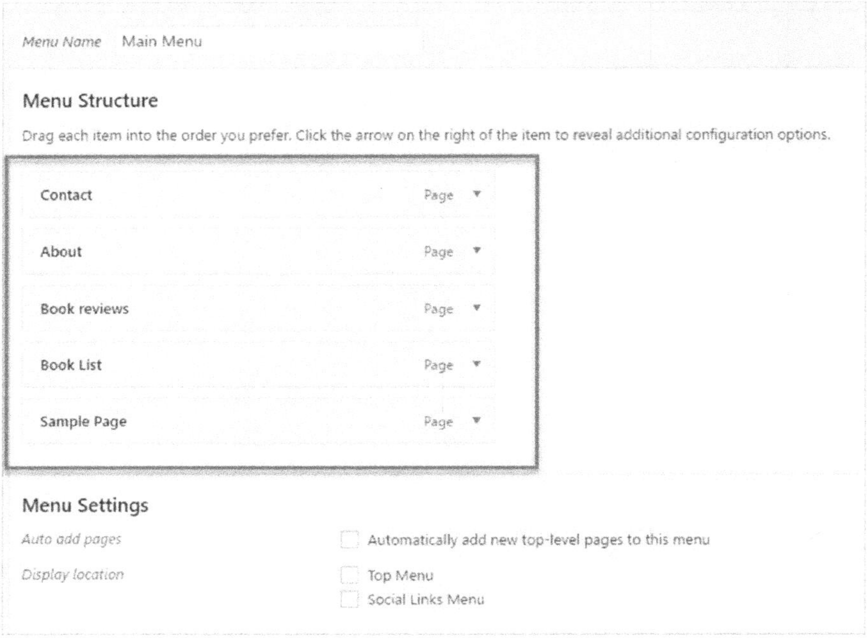

Menu Name   Main Menu

Menu Structure

Drag each item into the order you prefer. Click the arrow on the right of the item to reveal additional configuration options.

Contact	Page ▼
About	Page ▼
Book reviews	Page ▼
Book List	Page ▼
Sample Page	Page ▼

Menu Settings

Auto add pages   ☐ Automatically add new top-level pages to this menu

Display location   ☐ Top Menu
                            ☐ Social Links Menu

To change the **Navigation Label**, click on the down arrow on the right to expand the item, then enter the label you want for that item on the menu. For example, you can change the navigation label for the *Contact* page to *Contact U*s.

Contact Us   Page   ▲

Navigation Label

Contact Us

Move *Down one*

Original: Contact

Remove | Cancel

About   Page   ▼

Book reviews   Page   ▼

Book List   Page   ▼

Sample Page   Page   ▼

At the bottom of the page, you'll see the **Menu Settings** area. Here, you can select the option to automatically add new top-level pages to your new menu. This ensures that when you create a new page in future it will automatically be added to the menu.

When you are done, click on the **Create Menu** button to create the menu.

At the top of the screen, click on the **Manage Locations** tab.

Here you can select which menu to display for your **Top Menu** if you have created more than one menu for your site.

4.4 WordPress Headers

How you configure your header will depend on the theme you've installed. Most themes will allow you to select an image or logo for your header in the *General Settings* section of the theme options.

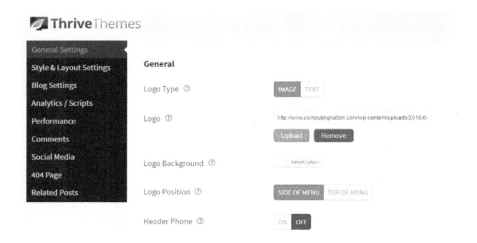

For other themes like Twenty Seventeen, you can access the header settings by clicking on **Appearance** and then **Header** in WP Admin. This takes you to a screen where you can customise the header by changing the image or adding a video.

CHAPTER 5: WORDPRESS PLUGINS

5.1 What Are Plugins?

Plugins are small scripts. That is, they are files with executable PHP code that enable you to add new functionality to your WordPress site. You use them to add functionality that is not available in the default installation of WordPress.

WordPress offers the essential features that most people will need for a blog or CMS site. WordPress has been highly optimised so that it loads very quickly, hence it does not include functionality that is non-essential for most people.

The good news is that you can customise it easily with plugins. If you want your site to have a particular feature to handle a specific task, there will surely be a plugin for it as others would have also thought of having that feature.

The great thing about plugins is that you don't need programming skills to use them. They're essentially like apps that you can download to your computer or smartphone for a specific task and they work out of the box.

Before content management systems like WordPress, to add a new functionality to your site you would need programming skills or hire a professional web developer, and that could cost a lot of money. So plugins are one of the things that make WordPress so popular.

5.2 Where To Get Plugins

Plugins are designed by different providers but they all need to adhere to the WordPress standard for their plugins to be compatible with WordPress. Many plugins are free. Oftentimes, people create them for their own use and then share them with the rest of the WordPress community by uploading them to WordPress.org.

Some plugins are supported by donations. Other plugins have two versions where the "light" version is provided for free and the premium version would have more features. If you like the free version and you want the extra features provided by the premium version then you would buy it.

WordPress.org is the official repository for WordPress plugins.

http://wordpress.org/extend/plugins/

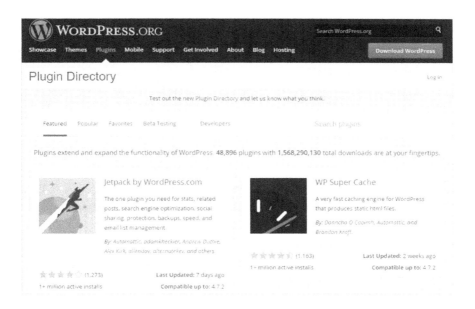

You can also access the site from within WP Admin by clicking on **Plugins**, and then **Add New**.

5.3 How To Find New Plugins

One of the best ways to find plugins for the feature you want is to search for it using **Google**. Type in *"WordPress plugin + [the feature you want]"* to get search results for plugins that meet your criteria.

You can also find new plugins from within WP Admin by using the search bar on the **Add Plugins** page. Usually, when you search for a plugin in WP Admin the most popular ones show up first. Before you install it, you can view the reviews, the number of active installs, when it was last updated, and if it is compatible with your version of WordPress.

If you see a feature on a WordPress site that you would like on your site and want to know what plugin provides the feature, you can actually do so by querying the site using a free tool on the internet.

Go to: http://www.wpthemedetector.com/

Copy and paste the URL of the site you want to check into the provided field and press enter.

You'll get:

1. The name of the main theme being used for the site.

2. Any child themes.

3. The plugins installed on the site.

This will give you a list of all the plugins used on the site. From the names of the plugins, you should be able to tell which one is providing the feature(s) you're after. You can then go to Google and search for the plugin. It could be a free plugin or a premium one.

For example, if you enter *http://www.createyourwebbiz.com* in the search bar of that site you'll see that **Jetpack by WordPress.com** and **WordPress SEO by Yoast** are two plugins installed on the site.

5.4 How To Install A Plugin

From WP Admin click on **Plugins** then click on **Add New**. This should display the **Add Plugins** screen. Use the **Search plugins** field to search for the plugin you want to install and then click on **Install Now**.

If you have downloaded a zip file for the plugin from the provider then click on **Upload Plugin**. Click on **Choose File** and then select the zip file you downloaded from the plugin provider. Then click on **Install Now**.

After installing a plugin you will usually get a new item on your WP

Admin menu that is the settings panel for the plugin. The plugin provider will usually provide all the help information you need to configure the plugin.

CHAPTER 6: WIDGETS AND SIDEBARS

6.1 Configuring Widgets

The main purpose of widgets is to provide an easy way of customising the sidebars and footers of your site with the addition of extra content. Widgets are usually placed on sidebars however you can place them anywhere on your site as long as you place them inside a widget area.

The number of widget areas on your site depends on the design of the theme you've installed. But generally, each theme has a widget area for the sidebar.

Typically, you can use a widget for the following:

1. The monthly archive list of your posts

2. A list of recent posts

3. A list of categories on your site

4. A tag cloud

5. The search box

6. Site adverts (entered as HTML or JavaScript in the widget)

7. A newsletter signup form

The Twenty Seventeen theme comes with three widget areas. One is the **Sidebar** and then you have two for the footer called **Footer 1** and **Footer 2**.

You can click on any of the widgets on the left-hand side of the screen and drag and drop them into a widget area.

You can also change the position of a widget you've dropped on a widget area by clicking on it and dragging it up or down.

For example, to display a calendar on my sidebar I would drag the **Calendar** widget and drop it on the **Sidebar** widget area, and click on **Save**. When I view the site, the calendar would now be in my sidebar.

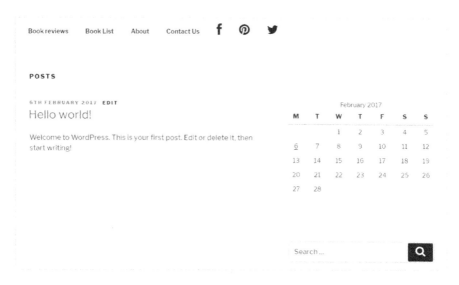

Enabling any kind of widget is very similar to this process. You just need to drag and drop the widget onto the area where you want it displayed. Once you have the widget in place you can adjust the settings and content. When you view your site, the contents of the widget will be rendered and displayed in that area.

The **Text** widget is what you use to place blocks of HTML or JavaScript code in your widget areas.

For example, if you have an ad or a sign-up form to display, the source would usually be a block of HTML text or JavaScript code. To place this on your sidebar, you drag the **Text** widget to your sidebar (or another widget area where you want the item displayed), and then you copy and paste the HTML or JavaScript into the **Content** field of the widget.

You could also give the widget a title by entering text in the **Title** field but this is optional.

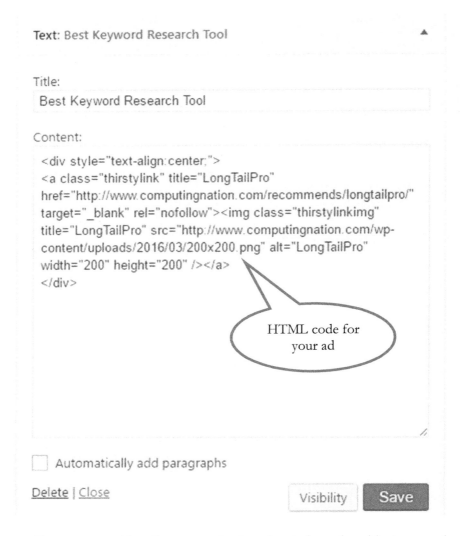

To remove a widget from your site, just drag it from the widget area and drop it on the other widgets on the left side of the screen. Alternatively, you can expand it and click on **Delete**.

Inactive Widgets

What if you do not want to delete the widget but you would like to deactivate it? At the bottom of the **Widgets** page, you will see a section for **Inactive Widgets**. This is the section where you can store widgets that you would like to remove from your site but you do not want to delete.

You may want to retain the settings you've made on the widget for use at another time.

So for example, you have a widget for a sign-up form on your sidebar and you want to temporarily deactivate this widget so it doesn't show on your site. Instead of deleting it you can drag it to the inactive widgets section. This means the code in it would be retained instead of deleted. Whenever you need to use this widget again or make use of any code inside it, you can simply drag it back to a widget area where you want it displayed.

6.2 How To Display A Different Sidebar

As you start adding pages and content to your WordPress site you may get to a point when you want different sidebars displayed on different pages. For example, you may have a sidebar that you use for your blog posts but you want a different one displayed for your Contact and About pages. The default installation of WordPress does not provide this feature however you can add it to your site with a free plugin.

There are many plugins that can do this but the one I currently use is called **Custom Sidebars**. You can download this free plugin from wordpress.org.

https://wordpress.org/plugins/custom-sidebars/

You can also search for "Custom Sidebars" in WP Admin and install it from there.

After installing and activating the plugin you will get a button on your Widgets screen that enables you to create a new sidebar.

Click on the button to create a new sidebar and enter the Name and Description. After creating a new sidebar it will show up next to the default sidebars in your theme and available for you to add widgets.

After adding the widgets to your sidebar you can choose where you want it displayed. To attach your custom sidebar to a post or page, go to that post or page and select the sidebar from the new **Sidebars** meta box that will now be on the right-side of the screen.

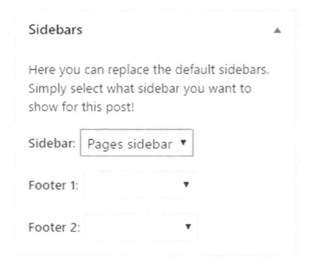

6.3 How To Create Social Media Links

You can also create a menu for social links/icons like Facebook, Twitter, Google+ etc. To create social media links you need to first install and activate the *Menu Social Icons* WordPress plugin at:

https://wordpress.org/plugins/menu-social-icons/

After installing and activating the plugin you'll get a **Social Icons** section added to the **Custom Links** menu section.

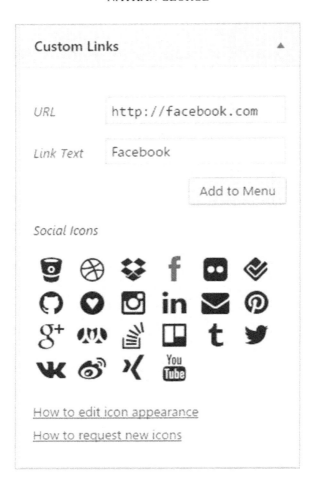

You can add the social media links to your main menu at the top of your site or on another menu that you can put in the footer of your site (if you install a theme where the layout allows a menu at the footer).

Menu Structure

Drag each item into the order you prefer. Click the arrow on the right of the item to reveal additic

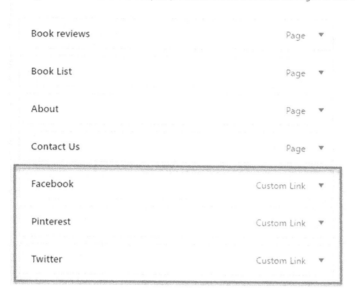

This is how the completed menu looks in this example.

CHAPTER 7: SECURING YOUR WEBSITE

7.1 How To Manually Backup Your Site

A few years back, you would need an FTP program like FileZilla to move files between your PC and your remote web host. Now we have the **File Manager** on cPanel (web host admin tool) which now allows you to directly transfer files between your PC and your remote web host.

You can still use an FTP program like FileZilla for file transfers, but I prefer using the File Manager as I find it to be faster and less of a hassle. That is, you do not need to install the FTP program on you PC and configure it with your FTP settings to connect to the remote web host.

In this chapter, I'll be using the File Manager for file transfers.

To manually take a backup of your WordPress site you just need to take a copy of two items:

1. The **wp-content** folder of your WordPress site.

2. The MySQL database of your WordPress site.

1. Take a copy the *wp-content* folder

In summary, these are the steps required to take a backup copy of your wp-content folder using File Manager:

1. Make a copy of the **wp-content** folder – remotely.

2. Compress the wp-content folder into a zip file - remotely (File Manager only allows you to download single files, not folders).

3. Download **wp-content.zip** to your PC.

Launch **File Manager** from cPanel and navigate to your home directory. Create a backup folder in your home directory (if you don't have one already). As you can see from the image below I've created a folder called *BackupNow*.

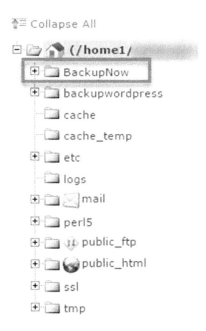

Next, navigate to your web root (usually *public_html*). Locate the folder for your website and select the **wp-content** folder.

Click on the **Copy** icon on the File Manager toolbar and specify your backup folder. For this example, it would be *BackupNow*.

Note: You can also copy the folder by holding down the **CTRL** key and then dragging and dropping it in the backup folder.

Next, select the wp-content folder on the right-hand side of the window and click on **Compress.**

Select *Zip Archive* (or whichever compression method you prefer) at the next prompt, then click on **Compress Files(s)**.

Once a compressed copy has been created (**wp-content.zip**), you can now download the file to your PC by selecting it and clicking on the **Download** toolbar icon.

2. Backup The MySQL Database

You first need to identify the name of your database (if you're not sure of the database your WordPress site is using).

To do this, launch **File Manager** on cPanel and locate the **wp-config.php** file being used by your WordPress installation. This would usually be in your web root (public_html) or a sub-folder under public_html if your site is an addon domain.

Select the file and click on the **View** icon on the File Manager toolbar to view the contents of the file in another window.

Scroll down to the section of the file with the MySQL settings, similar to this:

*// ** MySQL settings - You can get this info from your web host ** //*

/ ** The name of the database for WordPress */
*define('DB_NAME', **'wordpress'**);*

Look for the **DB_NAME** attribute. This will be the MySQL database for your WordPress site. In the example above, the database name is *wordpress*.

Next, you need to export a copy of the database to your PC using phpMyAdmin.

On cPanel, click on **phpMyAdmin** (it should be in the **database tools** category).

Select your database (the one you identified from your wp-config.php file) by clicking on the database name on the left of the screen.

Click on **Export** at the top of the screen. This should bring up a new screen that gives you a **Quick** or **Custom** export method.

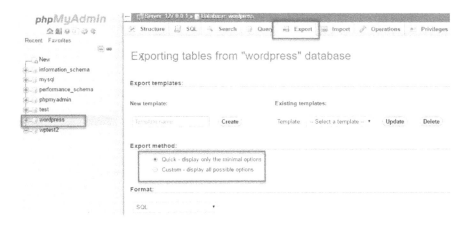

If you do not want to zip the file then just scroll down the page and click on the **Go** button to download the .sql file to your computer.

The file name would be in the format: *yourdatabasename.sql*.

If your site has a lot of data and you want to save the database as a zip file then follow these steps:

1. Click on **Custom – display all possible options**.

2. Ensure all tables are selected.

3. Change the **Compression** field to **zipped**.

4. Then scroll to the bottom of the screen and click the **Go** button.

The file will be downloaded to your PC. With these two items, you now have a full backup of your WordPress site.

7.2 Manually Restoring Your WordPress Site

To restore your WordPress contents folder, do the following:

1. Launch **File Manager** from cPanel and navigate to your home directory.

2. Click on the **Upload** button in File Manager and upload wp-content.zip (this is the zipped folder you downloaded when you backed up wp-content).

3. Select the file and click on **Extract** to unzip the folder.

4. Holding down the **CTRL** key, drag and drop the folder into your web root i.e. public_html (or the folder of your WordPress site if your site is an addon domain).

   Note: If you already have a folder named **wp-content** that you want to replace, rename the folder to **wp-contentOLD** first before copying the new one over.

To restore your MySQL database, do the following:

1. Launch **phpMyAdmin** from cPanel.

2. Create a new MySQL database and name it appropriately (see **chapter 1.6** for how to create a new MySQL database from cPanel).

3. Select the new database by clicking the database name in the list on the left of the screen.

4. Click on **Import** at the top of the screen to display another screen.

5. On the next screen, click on **Choose File** and select your backup file. This should be a .sql file or a .zip file.

6. Click **Go** to import the tables and content of the backup into the new database.

Ensure that your **wp-config.php** file (in the root folder of your website) is pointing to the new MySQL database. See instructions above for how to configure the settings of your wp-config.php file.

Launch your web browser and test that your site is running OK. If you've followed the steps as described above then your site should have been restored.

7.3 Automated Backups

It is a good idea to know how to manually backup your site in case a plugin fails hence we covered manual backups earlier in this chapter. However, to create scheduled backups that are automatically carried out, you need to use a plugin.

Keep in mind that some of the free backup plugins may not be perfect so you need to check what's actually being backed up. You may need to experiment with a few plugins to find one that suits your needs.

A free backup plugin that is very popular is **UpdraftPlus**. This plugin is one of the top-rated backup plugins in the WordPress.org plugin library and it has over 22 million downloads. It is also usually kept up to date with the latest version of WordPress.

UpdraftPlus simplifies backing up and restoring your site. The free version allows you to back up to a cloud drives like Amazon S3, Dropbox, Google Drive and restore your site with a single click.

The premium version offers more features which include, backing up to additional cloud drives like Microsoft OneDrive, Microsoft Azure, Google Cloud Storage and much more.

To install the plugin, in WP Admin, go to **Plugins > Add New**. Search for **UpdraftPlus.** Once found, click the **Install Now** button and then the **Activate** button.

Once the plugin is installed, navigate to the settings page of the plugin.

Under **Settings** there are two options which are initially set to manual:

*   File backup schedule

- Database backup schedule

The *file backup* will take a copy of the themes and plugins you installed on your site, while the *database backup* backs up your content. It is best to set both options so that both your files and content are backed up automatically. You can choose values from every couple of hours to monthly.

The interval you set will usually depend on how often you update your website. If you update your website daily, then you may want to choose daily backups for both. If you update your site weekly, then you may want to choose a weekly interval. Just make sure you don't set an interval that's shorter than necessary because the backup process does consume resources and can contribute to slowing down your site if done too often.

Next, choose the remote location you want to save the backup to. You have several options including Google Drive, Dropbox, Amazon S3, or even to email it to an email address.

The rest of the settings with this tool are self-explanatory. There is a premium option which gives you more features. I would recommend that you test the free version first to see if you like it before deciding if you want the additional features that the premium version offers.

7.4 Precautions With Login Credentials

Never use the username *Admin* for your site. That is way too easy to guess. And once a potential hacker knows your username then they only have your password left to figure out. Also, never use your admin username as the name you used to add posts to your website.

In WP Admin, under **Users > Your Profile**, enter a Nickname and select this name in the box **Display name publicly as**. Save this setting and this is the name that will be displayed with your posts, instead of your logon username.

Nickname *(required)*   Nathan

Display name publicly as   Nathan ▼

Always ensure you use a password that is difficult to guess. If you're having problems remembering too many passwords, then install a tool like LastPass that will store your online passwords for you in a secure vault so that you only need to remember one password.

7.5 Implementing Security With A Plugin

This is not absolutely necessary but if you want to explore adding security via plugins then you can try out Wordfence Security. Keep in mind that plugins do add additional overhead to your website so only install plugins that you consider necessary. It might be a good idea to consult your hosting provider first before installing a security plugin to ensure you're not installing something that's already been implemented by them globally on the server, hence redundant.

https://wordpress.org/plugins/wordfence/

Wordfence is one of the most popular security tools for WordPress. It works in preventing hackers from hacking into your site. Wordfence is free and open source however you can get premium services from the vendor to go with it like support, country blocking, password auditing, two-factor authentication etc.

AFTERWORD: NEXT STEPS

Thank you for buying and reading this book. I hope this book has been helpful to you whether you're creating a WordPress personal blog or a commercial website.

WordPress is a constantly evolving platform, with very regular updates, however, I have taken pains to ensure the information in *WordPress for Beginners* covered the core aspects of WordPress that have remained the same over the years. This ensures that this book will remain relevant even with later versions of WordPress.

Getting More Help with WordPress

https://wordpress.org/support/

The forums at WordPress.org are very useful when you have specific questions about WordPress. There are different forums for specific aspects of WordPress with a vibrant user community where users help each other with answers.

If you have a question, you can use the search function to perform a search on all the forums to see if your question has already been posted and answered. It is often the case that someone else encountered the same problems and it was discussed and answered. If you can't find an answer, then post your question in the relevant forum and you'll soon get help pointing you in the right direction.

If you found this book helpful I would be very grateful if you can take some time to share a review on Amazon.

Wishing you all the best with using WordPress and the success of your website.

APPENDIX: 22 TOP RATED WORDPRESS PLUGINS

The following are some of the best plugins for WordPress chosen from different categories of functionality. Some of them are free while others are premium but usually with a free trial.

Keep in mind that plugins generally add some overhead to your WordPress site regarding speed (apart from those specifically geared towards increasing loading performance). So, you need to choose wisely which plugins to install. I suggest you only install plugins you need and those that add value to your website i.e. the value they bring outweighs any performance overhead they may add.

1. Yoast SEO

https://wordpress.org/plugins/wordpress-seo/

Yoast SEO is one of the most popular Search Engine Optimisation (SEO) plugins for WordPress. It enables you to add metadata tags to your posts and it helps you to optimise your website as a whole. You can install the free version or upgrade to the premium version which offers more features and services.

2. W3 Total Cache

https://wordpress.org/plugins/w3-total-cache/

W3 Total Cache improves the performance of your site by allowing you to serve files that are compressed and cached to your visitors. This reduces the load time on your server, making your website faster. Faster websites are ranked higher by Googles hence this plugin will improve your site's

SEO.

3. Google XML Sitemaps

https://wordpress.org/plugins/google-sitemap-generator/

This plugin will generate a special XML sitemap that will allow search engines like Google, Bing, and Yahoo to better index your website. With such a sitemap it is easier for crawlers to see the full structure of your site and more efficiently retrieve it. This means your site will perform better in search engines making you more visible.

4. Wordfence Security

https://wordpress.org/plugins/wordfence/

Wordfence is one of the best security tools for WordPress. It has over 22 million downloads, making it the most popular security plugin available. It works in preventing hackers from hacking into your site. Wordfence is 100% free and open source. However, if you want more features then you can get premium services from the providers like support, country blocking, password auditing, two-factor authentication, and much more.

5. Contact Form 7

https://wordpress.org/plugins/contact-form-7/

Contact form 7 is the most popular contact form plugin for WordPress. It enables you to create a contact form on your site with just a few clicks and you can also manage multiple contact forms. The form supports CAPTCHA and Akismet spam filtering. The plugin is completely free but you can support the developer through donations.

6. NextGEN Gallery Plugin

https://wordpress.org/plugins/nextgen-gallery/

NextGEN is one of the top WordPress plugins for displaying a photo gallery. The free version of NextGEN offers two main display styles and two album styles. The display styles are slideshows and thumbnail galleries, and the album styles are compact and extended. You also get a wide array of options, including controlling size, timing, transitions, style, lightbox effects etc. If you want a photo gallery for your website then you should certainly give this plugin a try.

7. UpdraftPlus

https://wordpress.org/plugins/updraftplus/

UpdraftPlus simplifies backing up and restoring your site. The free version allows you to backup to a cloud drives like Amazon S3, Dropbox, Google Drive and restore your site with a single click. The premium version offers more features which include, backing up to additional cloud drives like Microsoft OneDrive, Microsoft Azure, Google Cloud Storage and much more.

UpdraftPlus is one of the best backup plugins on wordpress.org and it currently has over a million active installs. It has been widely tested and is one of the most reliable on the market.

8. Akismet

https://wordpress.org/plugins/akismet/

Akismet checks your comments and contact form submissions against a global database of spam to prevent your site from being spammed. It enables you to review the comment spam it catches on WP Admin. This free plugin is a must have if you want to prevent spam comments from flooding your website.

9. Jetpack by WordPress.com

https://wordpress.org/plugins/jetpack/

Jetpack provides many tools to keep any WordPress site secure, increase traffic, and better engage your readers. The tools provided include site stats and analytics, brute force attack protection, downtime and uptime monitoring, secured logins and two-factor authentication.

Most of Jetpack's features and services are free however you can also get affordable premium plans which include more features that include, support, advanced security and backup services, video hosting, site monetization, and SEO. At a minimum, all WordPress sites should have the free version of Jetpack.

10. iThemes Security

https://wordpress.org/plugins/better-wp-security/

iThems security provides over 30 ways for you to secure and protect your WordPress site. It is estimated that over 30,000 websites are hacked each day and this could be due to plugin vulnerability, weak passwords and obsolete software. iThemes Security works to fix common holes, prevent automated attacks and reinforce user credentials. You get the option of a free version and a pro version which offers more features like Two-Factor Authentication, Malware Scan Scheduling, Password Expiration, and Google reCAPTCHA.

11. Simple Membership

https://wordpress.org/plugins/simple-membership/

The simple membership plugin enables you to turn your WordPress site into a membership site. It means you can protect your posts and pages so that only members with login accounts can view the protected content.

This plugin lets you set up an unlimited amount of membership levels, for example, silver, platinum, and gold. This means your members can access different types of content on your site using the membership levels you create. This plugin is 100% free.

12. Yet Another Related Posts Plugin (YARPP)

https://wordpress.org/plugins/yet-another-related-posts-plugin/

With this plugin, you introduce your readers to related content on your site by displaying a list of related pages, posts and other content types related to the post they're currently reading.

This enables you to keep your readers engaged with relevant content which in turn would make them stay longer on your site.

13. Smush Image Compression and Optimization

https://wordpress.org/plugins/wp-smushit/

This incredibly powerful plugin allows you to resize, optimise, and compress all your images to improve your site's performance and SEO. One criterion Google uses to rank a page is the load time. So the faster your pages load, the higher they would rank it. You can set a max width and height and all large images will scale down as they're being compressed.

All the heavy lifting, in compressing the images, is done on remote servers provided by the plugin providers. So your server's performance is not affected by the processing required to compress the images. This plug-in is 100% free.

14. BJ Lazy Load

https://wordpress.org/plugins/bj-lazy-load/

This plugin replaces your images, post thumbnails, and other multimedia items with a placeholder during page loading, making your pages load faster. The items are only rendered in the sections of the pages that are visible on the screen. This means images are only downloaded when they need to be viewed. Again, this can improve your site's ranking as you pages load faster.

15. Duplicator

https://wordpress.org/plugins/duplicator/

Duplicator gives you the ability to migrate, copy, or clone your WordPress site from one location to another. This plugin can also be used as a simple backup tool. If you need to move your WordPress site then this tool will help to simplify the process immensely. You have the option of the basic version and a Pro version. The Pro version adds additional features like schedule backups, backups cloud storage, multisite support, email notifications, and much more.

16. Broken Link Checker

https://wordpress.org/plugins/broken-link-checker/

This plugin will check your posts, comments and other content for broken links and notify you if any are found. Once installed, the plugin will go through your content and bookmarks to look for any broken links. This may take from a few minutes to a few hours depending on how large your site is. If broken links are found they would show up on a new tab in WP Admin. This plugin helps you to keep your site up to date and ensure all links on your site work, which in turn helps to improve what your visitors experience.

17. Disable Comments

https://wordpress.org/plugins/disable-comments/

This plugin will allow you to globally disable comments on any type of content (posts, pages, attachments, etc.). This means that the settings cannot be overridden for individual posts. This can be very useful for multisite installations as you can disable comments on the entire network.

The default installation of WordPress allows you to selectively disable comments on individual posts so if that is all you need then you don't need this plugin. Only use this plugin if you do not want comments at all on your site.

18. Redirection

https://wordpress.org/plugins/redirection/

Redirection is a WordPress plugin that allows you to manage 301 redirections and keep track of 404 errors without needing to access your server's .htaccess file. This plugin is especially useful if you are migrating pages from one site to another or if you change the directory of your WordPress installation. This plugin is 100% free.

19. TablePress

https://wordpress.org/plugins/tablepress/

TablePress allows you to quickly create and manage tables on your site.

The plugin provides a spreadsheet-like interface that enables you to edit data without any coding. You can embed the tables into your content or widgets with a simple shortcode.

You can enter any type of data and even formulas that will be evaluated. The table features allow site visitors to sort and filter the data to provide different views. You can also import and export data from/to Excel, CSV, HTML, and JSON files.

20. Advanced Custom Fields

https://wordpress.org/plugins/advanced-custom-fields/

This plugin gives you the flexibility to create custom fields for your website like other content management systems. You can list items on your site using data fields specific to that type. For example, you may want an easy way to list books on your site. With this plugin, you can create fields for the book title, author, book description, publication date etc. So when you add a new book you would have specific fields for the data you want to store about the book.

You can visually create your fields, select from multiple input types, assign your fields to multiple edit pages, and much more. It is one of the best WordPress plugins for custom fields.

21. Display Widgets

https://wordpress.org/plugins/display-widgets/

This plugin allows you to change the widgets that are displayed on your sidebar for different pages. There are many plugins that allow you to create different sidebars to use for different pages. However, with this plugin, you do not need to create multiple sidebars with duplicate widgets. Instead, it adds checkboxes to each widget, allowing you to select on which pages you want to show or hide the widget.

22. Social Media and Share Icons (Ultimate Social Media)

https://wordpress.org/plugins/ultimate-social-media-icons/

This plugin is the most popular social media plugin with over 70,000 active installs. The plugin allows you to add social media share icons to your site like RSS, Email, Facebook, Twitter, LinkedIn, Google+, Pinterest, Instagram, Youtube etc. It also allows you to upload custom icons of your choice. This plugin is 100% free.

INDEX

DID YOU LIKE THIS BOOK?

You can make a big difference

Reviews are the most powerful tools for independent authors like myself when it comes to getting attention for our books. We don't have the financial muscle of the big publishers making the New York Times lists. I can't take out full page ads in the newspaper or put posters on the subway (not yet anyway).

However, I do have something much more powerful and effective than that. A bunch of happy and loyal readers.

Honest reviews help bring my books to the attention of other readers.

If this book has been useful to you I would be very grateful if you could spend just five minutes leaving a review on this book's Amazon page (it can be as short as you like).

You can go directly to the reviews page with the weblink below.

US: https://amzn.to/2JioxMI

UK: https://amzn.to/2Ek0WHM

Thank you very much.

ABOUT THE AUTHOR

Nathan George is a computer science graduate and worked for several years in the IT services industry as a web developer before entering the dot com world to create and run his own commercial websites. He currently runs several profitable niche websites all powered by WordPress. As an author, he has written several technical books and help guides.

OTHER BOOKS BY AUTHOR

Keyword Research

How To Find And Profit From Low Competition Long Tail
Keywords + 33 Profitable Niches Analysed

Keyword Research will teach you practical ways of finding out what people are
actively searching for online and spending money on. You'll learn how to
find profitable niches online to enter and how competitive they are. This
knowledge will dramatically increase your likelihood of success in doing
business online.

Available at Amazon:

http://www.amazon.com/gp/product/B00U8ZY5IK

Digital Product Blueprint

How To Turn Your Knowledge, Passion Or Expertise Into Information Products You Can Sell Online

Creating your own information product is currently one of the fastest ways to start making money online today. You don't even need to create a website to start earning online these days. *Digital Product Blueprint* provides a step by step approach that covers the process of creating your digital product, where to sell it online, and how to promote and market your product.

Available at Amazon

https://www.amazon.com/dp/B06XDPHTH3

Convert Your Text To Audio

Boost Your Reading Capacity And Speed Using Free Tools Like Audacity

If you don't have the time to stop and read as much as you would like to, *Convert Your Text To Audio* will show you a method you can use to read more books, faster, and with less effort. This book provides a step-by-step guide for how to convert any kind of digital text material into MP3 audio files that you can listen to on the go. We live in the information age and our ability to assimilate information fast is increasingly becoming critical for success. Reading is one of the best investments you can make in yourself.

Available at Amazon:

https://www.amazon.com/dp/B01EBLTZCC

www.ingramcontent.com/pod-product-compliance
Lightning Source LLC
LaVergne TN
LVHW052309060326
832902LV00021B/3793